Rugby Made Simple
(For Baffled Spectators)

Val Anderson
(with cartoons by Rupert Besley)

An environmentally friendly book printed and bound in England by www.printondemand-worldwide.com

This book is made entirely of chain-of-custody materials

Val Anderson

FastPrint Publishing

www.fast-print.net/store.php

RUGBY MADE SIMPLE
(FOR BAFFLED SPECTATORS)
Copyright © Val Anderson 2014

All rights reserved

No part of this book may be reproduced in any form by photocopying or any electronic or mechanical means, including information storage or retrieval systems, without permission in writing from both the copyright owner and the publisher of the book.

The right of Val Anderson to be identified as the author of this work has been asserted by her in accordance with the Copyright, Designs and Patents Act 1988 and any subsequent amendments thereto.

A catalogue record for this book is available from the British Library

ISBN 978-178456-109-3

First published 2014 by
FASTPRINT PUBLISHING
Peterborough, England.

Rugby Made Simple

Contents

Introduction	5
The Team	7
Scoring	13
The Golden Rule, the Mystery of the Scrum and the Strange Case of the Knock-On	17
Tackling and the Subtle Difference between a Ruck and a Maul	23
The Line-Out (When, Where, Why, Who and How?)	27
The Offside Rule	31
Playing Advantage	37
Penalties and How to Play Them	39
Referee Hand Signals	43
Frequently Asked Questions	51
A Brief History of Rugby Union	55

Val Anderson

Introduction

"Rugby is a game for the mentally deficient... That is why it was invented by the British. Who else but an Englishman could invent an oval ball?" – Peter Pook

"The women sit, getting colder and colder, on a seat getting harder and harder, watching oafs, getting muddier and muddier." – Virginia Graham

This book is written for anyone who watches rugby union matches without understanding the rules. In particular it is written for the dedicated parents of blossoming players who spend hours standing on the sidelines to encourage their offspring. These heroic supporters regularly brave rain, wind and freezing cold to watch their progeny pound up and down the pitch, wash endless loads of muddy kit and watch anxiously for possible injuries.

Technically speaking, rugby union has "laws" rather than "rules" but in the interests of simplicity I have referred to "rules" throughout this book.

At its best rugby is dramatic, fast-paced and often mesmerising to watch. However it is a highly technical and complex game which is hard to appreciate without an adequate grasp of the rules. My hope is that this book will help every baffled rugby spectator and increase their enjoyment of this great sport.

Note:

This is not intended to be a definitive or exhaustive guide to the rules – indeed such a thing is impossible as they continue to evolve each year. However it should give you enough information to work out the gist of what is going on amidst the melee of writhing bodies, regular stoppages and bewildering formations.

Chapter One
The Team

"Remember that rugby is a team game; all 14 of you make sure you pass the ball to Jonah." (Fax to the All Blacks before the 1995 World Cup semi-final.)

"Rugby is a game for big buggers. if you're not a big bugger, you get hurt. I wasn't a big bugger but I was a fast bugger and therefore I avoided the big buggers." – Spike Milligan

Here's a description of a stereotypical rugby team – what the coach dreams of sending out onto the pitch. However it may not bear any resemblance to the rugby team you are watching!

Before we set off you need to grasp that numbers 1-8 form the **"forwards"** and make up the **"scrum"** and **"line-out"** whilst numbers 9-15 are the **"backs".** The mysteries of these two terms will be revealed as you read on. You can see the numbers on the back of the shirts.

1. Loose-head prop – so called because only one side of his head is locked into the scrum. Big and beefy, he is often referred to as a "meathead" and rarely has a neck.

2. Hooker – it's an unfortunate name but refers to the fact that he "hooks" the ball out of the scrum with his feet. His other job is to throw the ball in a line-out. Usually small but strong.

3. Tight-**head prop** – he is locked in the centre of the scrum on both sides. Another "meathead", he needs to be a solid and immovable object.

4. and 5. Locks or second row – These two form the second row of the scrum. Tall and slim, they are the flagpoles of the team and need reliable leg muscles to add power to the scrum.

Rugby Made Simple

6. and 7. Blind-side flanker and open-side flanker. They "flank" the scrum and are the first to break away once the ball is out. As the fastest forwards they provide essential support and have a high contact rate. (Head protection highly recommended!)

8. Number eight – adds power to the scrum at the back. Generally a large and strong runner with good ball handling skills.

9. Scrum half – usually the smallest member of the team, he links the forwards and the backs. Needs a loud voice to yell at the team and good ball passing skills. He does NOT form part of the scrum itself but puts the ball into the scrum and then retrieves it once it has been heeled out by the hooker.

10. Fly half – known as the play maker, he needs good decision making skills as he chooses to either kick the ball or pass it to his team mates. Arguably the most important position on the pitch. (Sometimes called stand-off).

11. Left wing – together with right wing he is the fastest member of the team expected to finish try scoring opportunities.

12. Outside centre – a well built figure with good ball retention skills and a solid defence. Similar to the inside centre (below) but generally a bit faster.

13. Inside centre – stands near to the fly-half and good at tactical decisions. Both centres are similar to wingers but have higher defensive responsibilities.

14. Right wing – as for left wing (above), dependent on having the ball passed out to him before weaving his way to the touchline. Nimble, fast and slippery.

15. Full-back – the last line of defence with great one-to-one tackling skills. Needs to be a good kicker to lob the ball safely away from the try line.

At the end of this chapter you will find a pitch showing the names of the players and where they usually stand on the pitch.

So What Are They Trying To Do...?

It may look like organised murder but they are actually trying to either ground the ball on or over the try line or kick it through the goal posts. This gives them points and the team with the most points wins. Simple! Or not...

Rugby Made Simple

Diagram Of Rugby Pitch Showing Player Positions

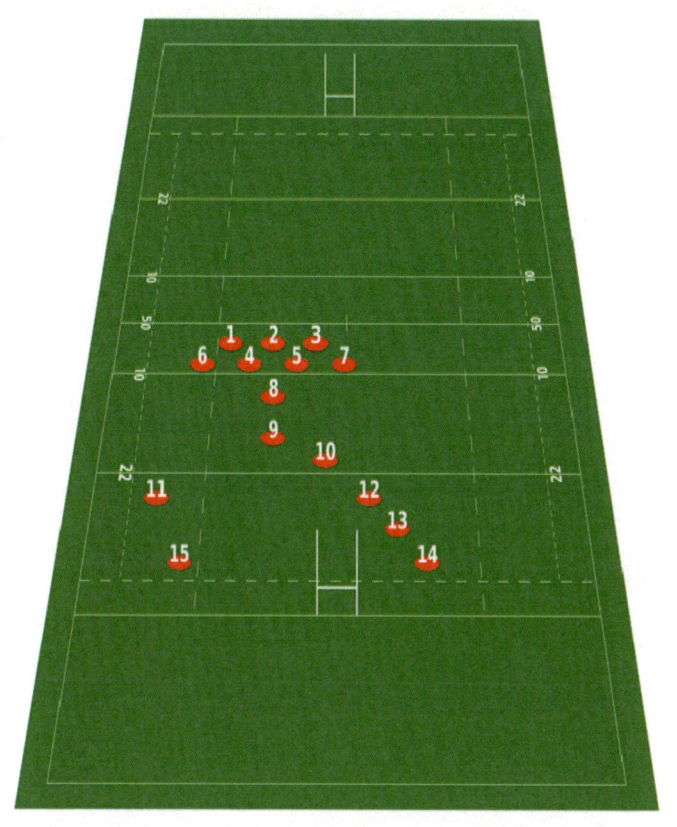

1: Loose-head prop, 2: Hooker, 3: Tight-head Prop, 4: Lock, 5: Lock, 6: Blind-side flanker, 7: Open-side flanker, 8: Number eight, 9: Scrum half, 10: Fly half, 11: Left wing, 12: Outside centre, 13: Inside centre, 14: Right wing, 15: Full back

This work is licensed under a Creative Commons Attribution Share-Alike 2.0 Licence. (https://creativecommons.org/licenses/by-sa/2.0/deed.en) Copyright (C) Titimaster

Val Anderson

Chapter Two
Scoring

"No leadership, no ideas. Not even enough imagination to thump someone in the line-up when the ref wasn't looking." – J.P.R. Williams (1984) when Wales lost 28-9 against Australia

"The first half is invariably much longer than the second. This is partly because of the late kick-off but is also caused by the unfitness of the referee." – Michael Green

This is relatively easy so let's start with that.

- A try scores five points
- A goal converted from a try scores two points
- A goal scored from a penalty kick or a drop kick scores three points.

A try is not really a "try" in the common meaning of that word but a successful score achieved when a player "grounds" the ball on or beyond the try line. The ball is **grounded** by the player holding the ball down or falling on the ball with the upper part of his body.

This can be done by a single player running through the defence or by a group pushing over the try line and grounding the ball. It's often hard to see whether the ball has been properly grounded causing heated arguments between spectators and much head scratching from the referee.

A goal is scored by kicking the ball over the crossbar and between the goalposts from a kicking tee.

A player can score a goal from a "drop kick" at any time but goals are more often scored as "conversions" – ie the right to convert a try and score two more points.

Hot Tip

You'll know if there's been a try if the referee raises one arm straight above his head.

A goal is signalled by a touch judge raising his flag after the kick.

Make sure you keep score mentally – the chances are that fifty per cent of the crowd won't have a clue what it is and the other half will have got it wrong. Scoreboards are not always available.

Diagram of rugby pitch showing dimensions, goal area and try line

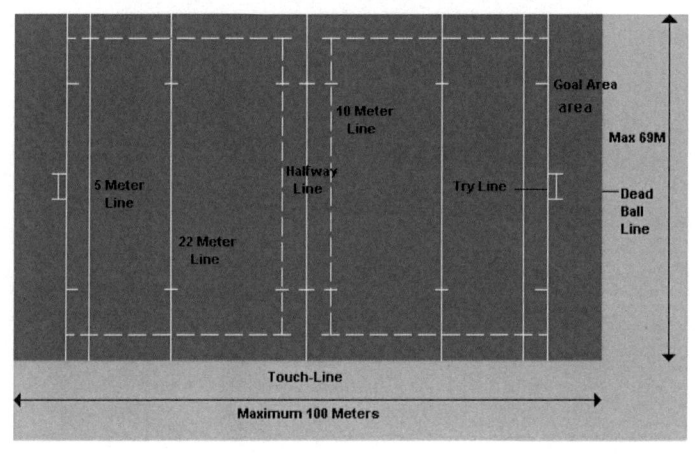

Copyright (C) Deadmanwalking Wikicommons.

Val Anderson

Chapter Three

The Golden Rule, the Mystery of the Scrum and the Strange Case of the Knock-On

"I think you enjoy the game more if you don't know the rules. Anyway, you're on the same wavelength as the referees." – Jonathan Davies, A Question of Sport BBC TV (1995)

"The Holy Writ of Gloucester Rugby Club demands: first, that the forwards shall win the ball; second, that the forwards shall keep the ball; and third, the backs shall buy the beer." – *Doug Ibbotson*

We are going to take a look at rugby's central rule, the scrum that usually follows from the breach of that rule and the complexities of the "knock-on". (The "knock-on" is when a player accidentally knocks the ball forward).

The Golden Rule

The ball must only be passed or knocked _backwards_ but it can be kicked _forwards._

Odd? Absolutely, but this is rugby and believe me, it gets even odder...

Pause a moment to grasp this central idea and remember that adverse consequences result from infringements of this rule. Get this, memorise it and you've got the big one.

Now for what happens when it is broken.

Forward pass – the referee will award a scrum with the "put-in" to the other team. The "put-in" is the right to place the ball into the scrum.

Knock-on – if this was accidental the opposition will be awarded a scrum. If it was intentional then the opposition will be awarded a penalty.

This is a good moment to describe a scrum as it almost invariably follows on from a breach of the Golden Rule.

The Scrum

It's worth spending a bit of time on this as it's a very technical aspect of the game and the cause of much stress to the referee as he tries to organise 16 belligerent players into the correct formation, remember a myriad of special rules and ensure that the scrum ritual is properly carried out.

Think back to Chapter One and the description of players 1-8. These hunks have the job of binding themselves together and forming a driving wall of muscle against the opposition who are in a similar formation. This traditionally consists of a 3-4-1 arrangement, ie the front row has three men, the second row has four and number eight is on his own at the back. Each band "engages" with the other by crouching down and interlocking in a strictly prescribed way forming a closed circle and a tunnel between the legs of each side.

Diagram of scrum formation:
1. Loose-head prop, 2. Hooker, 3. Tight-head prop, 4. Lock, 5. Lock, 6. Blind-side Flanker, 7. Open-side flanker, 8. Number eight.

Copyright (C) Shudde. Wikicommons.

As soon as the scrum is formed the scrum half puts the ball into the circle at which point it may be played. That means each side can start pushing against the other and try to win the ball. The team putting in the ball generally wins the scrum by pushing over the ball and allowing their hooker to heel the ball out the back by which time the scrum half will have run round the back to collect it. The opposing side will try to "wheel" the scrum – push it round sideways and disrupt possession of the ball.

There are a host of subsidiary rules about scrums including instructions to the scrum half on how and where to put the ball in, what a player can or can't do whilst locked in the scrum and penalties for collapsing a scrum or lifting an opponent off his feet. Leave these to the referee or buy a more advanced version of rugby rules if you're really keen.

Hot Tip

Remember that the whole point of a scrum is to get the ball back into play after a stoppage caused by a minor infringement and the non-infringing team will be awarded the right to put the ball into the scrum.

The Knock-On

You'll see plenty of these on a wet and windy day as slippery fingers drop the ball and misjudged passes bounce off team mates. Most fumbles with the ball result in a knock-on drawing sighs of exasperation from the coach.

Any forward movement of the ball towards the enemy line apart from a kick counts as a knock-on with one important exception. If a player blocks a kick with his body without actually trying to catch the ball it's NOT a knock-on. (The fancy term for this is a charge-down). Most knock-ons are accidents and result in a scrum.

(Note that if a player knocks the ball forward and catches it again before it hits the ground (or hits another player) it isn't a knock-on.)

Val Anderson

Chapter Four
Tackling and the Subtle Difference Between a Ruck and a Maul

"I prefer rugby to soccer. I enjoy the violence in rugby, except when they start biting each other's ears off." – Elizabeth Taylor (1972)

" Serious sport has nothing to do with fair play, it is bound up with hatred, jealousy, boastfulness, disregard for all rules and sadistic pleasure in witnessing violence; in other words it is war minus the shooting." – George Orwell

Tackling

This is the really fun stuff that makes it legal to roll around in the mud, get totally filthy, beat up the opposition and still get applause from the crowd. Unfortunately there are a number of rules which will thwart any ambitions to completely annihilate the boy who pinched your lunch money or settle old scores with an enemy. Here's a list of the main things a tackler and the tackled player must avoid doing:

Don'ts for the Tackler

Stamp on, trample, punch or kick another player.

Make a high tackle (which means contact above the shoulders). This one is a big no-no for obvious safety reasons and may result in the offender being sent off.

Hang onto the player who has been tackled. The tackler must roll quickly away from the player and the ball.

Don'ts for the Person Tackled

Continue to hang onto the ball after being grounded. This is a frequent error as players instinctively hang onto a hard won ball and fail to release it quickly. A player lying on the ground is effectively out of the game and cannot even touch the ball after releasing it until back on his feet again.

Rucks and Mauls

If a player carrying the ball manages to stay on his feet and a general melee ensues with one or more other players closing in on him, it's called a **maul**.

However if the ball is on the ground and a heaving mass of bodies converges on it, its called a **ruck.**

The subtle difference between a **ruck** and a **maul** is that the ball is on the ground in a **ruck** but remains held by a standing player in a **maul**.

(Remember – in the muck makes it a ruck but standing tall makes it a maul). Being able to tell the difference is sure to impress!

Top Tip

You'll see the referee dancing round the ruck or maul until he decides that the ball has become unplayable at which point he will blow his whistle and declare a scrum.

Val Anderson

Chapter Five
The Line-Out (When, Where, Why, Who and How?)

"The job of Welsh coach is like a minor part in a Quentin Tarantino film: you stagger on, you hallucinate, nobody seems to understand a word you say, you throw up, you get shot." – Mark Reason

This is slightly more comprehensible to spectators than a scrum but it's actually just as complicated with varying numbers of players involved, detailed rules on distances and how the ball can be thrown in. The broad idea is for the thrower to throw the ball in a straight line and for each team to toss a man into the air to catch it. Like the scrum, the team with the right to throw in are expected to win the line-out but that frequently goes wrong.

When?

A line-out is taken whenever the ball is crosses the touchline – it can be knocked or kicked over the line or the player holding the ball can be forced over by the opposition. (The touchline is the line marking the boundary down either side of the pitch). The right to throw the ball in is given to the team who didn't put it out.

Where?

Tricky one. Pay attention. If a player is tackled out of play with the ball, the line out is taken from where this happened If the ball is kicked directly into touch and doesn't touch the ground before it goes over, the line-out is taken opposite the place where the player kicked, ie it gains no ground for the team! However if it hits the ground before going over the line then the line-out is opposite the place where it went out – that's a successful kick.

BUT – there are two vital exceptions to this rule. First, a player can kick from within his own 22meter (that's the bit near the goal) directly into touch and gain ground for his team provided he didn't personally take the ball into that area. The usual scenario is for the full-back to catch the ball and then wellie it as far down the pitch as he can.

The second exception is a penalty kick which can be taken from anywhere on the field. Note that in this case the kicker's team will also get the throw-in.

Why?

Like the scrum the purpose of the line-out is to restart the game quickly and fairly after a minor infringement by throwing it in at the place where it crossed the touchline.

Who?

A line-out has between two and eight players from each team, the number being decided by the team throwing in. Like the scrum the forwards (numbers 1-8) participate in this ritual.

How?

That's another difficult one. The thrower stands behind the touchline, the receivers must be between five and fifteen meters from touch and one meter apart. It's usually the hooker who throws in and he is supposed to throw it straight down the line giving both sides an equal chance of catching the ball. In practice this doesn't happen as the thrower will yell a coded message giving secret information about how far he will lob it and who he is expecting to catch it.

Is That All?

Well, no. There are a host of rules about barging, obstruction, peeling-off and where the other players must stand. Leave them to the ref and bear in mind that like the scrum, the line-out is frequently shambolic, bad-tempered and has to be redone. This is especially true towards the end of a game when exhaustion sets in and tempers are frayed.

Chapter Six
The Offside Rule

"In 1823, William Webb Ellis first picked up the ball in his arms and ran with it. And for the next 156 years forwards have been trying to work out why." – Sir Tasker Watkins

Offside

Take a deep breath and concentrate – this is the really hard stuff. Bone up on it and your confidence levels as a spectator will rise. You'll be able to yell "offside" with the best of them.

Offside in Open Play

The best way to understand this is to imagine what the game would look like if the offside rule didn't exist. Players could station themselves anywhere on the pitch – standing on their opponents goal line would be a great spot – and wait until the ball gets kicked towards them. Scoring tries would be simple – get ahead and wait for the ball to come to you. Rugby would start to look like football (heaven forbid!).

The offside rule prevents this from happening and neutralises a player who is standing **in front of his teammate who has the ball**. There are two main scenarios in open play where this can happen so let's imagine a player called "Tom" for the sake of convenience:

1) If one of Tom's team mates kicks the ball forward while Tom is **in front** of him, Tom would be deemed offside. Tom can't play the ball or obstruct an opponent. He can't move towards the ball or even towards the enemy waiting to play the ball. All Tom can do is get out of the way fast and stand at least 10

metres away from where the ball lands or from the opponent waiting for the ball.

2) Additionally, if the opposition kicks the ball to a player behind Tom, then Tom would be offside and would be out of the game until he gets behind his team mate who has the ball.

Getting Onside Again

We've talked about being offside but how does a player get onside again? Let's go back to Tom. He is standing offside and is effectively out of the game and must wait to be put on side by his own team or by his opponents.

Played onside by his own team

- A teammate runs in front of Tom carrying the ball.
- Tom runs behind any of his onside teammates or any of these teammates run ahead of Tom.
- A teammate who was behind Tom when he kicked the ball runs ahead of him.

Played onside by the enemy

- If Tom is ahead of a teammate who kicks the ball and the ball ends up in enemy hands then Tom will be onside again once that opponent runs 5 metres with the ball, kicks it or passes it.

If Tom messes up and infringes the rule, the enemy will be awarded a penalty kick or a scrum (at their option).

So far so good but there are variations on the rule for scrums, rucks and mauls and that's before you get to the rules about getting onside again. Finish this chapter if you want the more detailed rules, otherwise just remember that the offside rule ensures that a player cannot get ahead of the ball if it's held by his team and then wait for it.

Offside at the Scrum

There are two distinct rules – one for the scrum-halves and one for everyone else.

The offside line for scrum-halves runs through the ball itself. For everyone else the offside line is an imaginary line drawn through the foot of the last player in the scrum. Think of it as a battleline – no player can get in front of his teammates in the scrum.

Offside for Rucks and Mauls

Fortunately the rules for being offside at a ruck or maul are the same. In either case players who are not involved must stand **behind** their teammates in the ruck or maul or, if they choose to join it, they must join in at the **back** of their team.

The regular error is to join in from the side of the crowd – an often irresistible temptation for the impetuous and determined but once again it will result in a penalty kick or a scrum – assuming the referee has noticed!

Val Anderson

Chapter Seven
Playing Advantage

"The advantage law is the best law in rugby, because it lets you ignore all the others for the good of the game." – Derek Robinson

"New Zealand rugby is a colourful game since you get all black ... and blue" – Anon

One of the easier rules. It's designed to keep the game alive after an offence or foul. If one side commits an offence and the other side gains an advantage from this the referee will allow the game to continue.

The common example is where a player knocks on but the other side grabs the ball. Instead of blowing his whistle the referee will overlook the offence because it has given an advantage to the non-infringing team.

This rule covers almost all the game – every time an opponent makes a mistake the other side can profit from it. However it doesn't apply if the ball touches the referee or in certain situations in the scrum.

You'll hear people shouting "play to the whistle" which is advice to carry on playing even though a rule has been broken. One of the challenges for a referee is to keep the game moving with as few stoppages as possible and the advantage law is designed to achieve this.

Top Tip

If you notice an infringement and wonder why the ref hasn't blown his whistle, it's probably because he is waiting to see if the other side has gained an advantage from the error.

Chapter Eight
Penalties and How to Play Them

In Chapter Three we talked about the scrum and how it results from a **mino**r infringement of the rules such as a forward pass or an accidental knock-on. What happens if there is a **major** infringement, what's the difference anyway and how can you tell if it's been a major or minor one?

As a very rough rule, a minor offence is accidental, doesn't threaten life and limb and doesn't offend the notion of fair play. On the other hand, a major offence generally involves an element of deliberate breach, gratuitous violence or bad sportsmanship.

<u>Major infringements</u> include:-

Dangerous play such as high or late tackles

Foul play (stamping on body parts, tripping someone up, ear chomping etc.)

Obstruction (eg deliberately shielding a team mate by blocking a tackle or pushing an opponent out of the way as he runs for the ball)

Deliberate knock-ons

Dissent (ie – arguing with the referee)

Misconduct (eg taunting an opponent after scoring or deliberately wasting time)

Failing to release the ball after being tackled

Entering a ruck or maul from the side

Deliberately collapsing a scrum

(There are plenty of others but these are the common ones).

If it's been a minor offence, the game will restart with a scrum. If it's a **major** offence then the non-offending team is awarded a **penalty** and has a choice of remedy. Their captain will choose one of the following options:-

1. Kick for points. (This is perfect if the ball is near enough the goal and will provide three points)

2. Scrum. (Useful if the goal line is near, time is running out and the team needs more than three points to win. A successful scrum in this situation offers the chance to score a try and gain another seven points).
3. Kick for touch (The obvious choice if the ball is a long way from the goal line. A good kick will gain ground for the team and result in a line-out to the same team).
4. Tap'n'go. (ie the ball holder will tap the ball with his foot and resume normal play. This a tactical decision – it is the fastest way to restart the game and can take the opposition by surprise. A good choice if the opposition looks disorganised and tired.)

Hot Tip

If the referee holds up a yellow card it means that player has to spend 10 minutes in the sin bin. If it's a red card then he is off for the whole match. Either card means that the offence was really serious, there has been a repeated infringement (or that the referee is in a foul mood).

Val Anderson

Chapter Nine
Referee Hand Signals

The referee has a bewildering number of hand and arm signals at his disposal each of which indicates an infringement or an instruction to the players. This constitutes a kind of sign language known only to initiates into the highest order of this religion. In fact there are over forty coded messages ranging from awarding a try to calling for a doctor. The illustrations below should help you to decipher the more common of these.

Try Given/Penalty Try

The referee will clearly raise one arm straight above his head. His back will be towards the dead ball line.

Kick at Goal Successful

It's usually a linesman standing behind the goal posts who will raise a flag.

Knock-On.

The referee will raise his arm with an open palm and move it backwards and forwards.

Forward Pass.

The referee will pretend to pass an imaginary ball forward.

Rugby Made Simple

Scrum Awarded.

The referee stands with shoulders parallel with touch-line and his arm horizontal pointing towards the team to put-in the ball.

Wheeling the Scrum More Than 90 Degrees.

The referee will rotate his finger above his head. The scrum will be reset.

Prop Pulling down Opponent.

The referee clenches his fist and bends his arm with a downwards pulling motion. It's an offence to collapse a scrum.

Touch and Team to Throw in

The touch judge will stand where the ball went out, raise the flag and indicate the team to throw in.

High Tackle.

The referee's hand will move horizontally in front of his neck.

Not Releasing Ball Immediately in Tackle

The referee will pull his arms to his chest as if clutching a ball.

Rugby Made Simple

Penalty Kick.

The referee's shoulders are parallel with the touch-line. His arm is angled up, pointing towards the non-offending team.

Offside at Scrum Ruck or Maul.

The referee stands with his shoulders parallel to the touch-line. His arm hangs straight down, swinging in an arc along off-side line.

Advantage.

The referee's arm is held outstretched, waist high, towards the non-offending team, for a few seconds.

Stamping.

The referee will pretend to stamp.

Throw-In at Line-Out not Straight.

The referee will stand parallel with the touchline and hold his hand above his head.

Coming in from the Side at a Ruck or Maul.

The referee holds his hand and arm horizontally and moves it sideways.

Handling Ball in Ruck or Scrum

The referee holds his hand at ground level, making sweeping actions, as if handling the ball.

Val Anderson

Frequently Asked Questions

"Rugby is a hooligans' game played by gentlemen." *Winston Churchill*

"On female rugby teams – Everybody thinks we should have moustaches and hairy arses, but in fact you could put us all on the cover of Vogue." *– Helen Kirk (1987)*

Who Invented the Game?

Folklore alleges that rugby was born in 1823 when a pupil at Rugby School, namely William Webb Ellis, got fed up with playing football, picked up the ball and ran with it. There isn't a lot of evidence to substantiate this view but if you visit Rugby School you'll find a plaque on the school pitch recording this momentous sporting occasion. The Rugby World Cup is called the "William Webb Ellis Trophy".

Why is the Rugby Ball Oval?

They were originally made from inflated pigs bladders (honestly!) and so took on that shape. A local cobbler called William Gilbert produced the first ball for Rugby School and his home is now The Rugby Football Museum. His name has been immortalised on rugby balls still used today. The oval shape has become more pronounced over time and is easier to hold than a spherical shape. The weight and circumference are strictly prescribed. Smaller balls are used for younger players.

Why is a Try Called a Try?

Originally a "try" did not carry any points at all but allowed the successful team to "try to score a goal" by kicking the ball over the cross bar and between the posts. It was not until the late 1880s that points could be scored with a try.

What are the Dimensions of a Rugby Pitch?

It's a maximum of 70 metres wide and a goal to goal length of 100 metres. The in-goal area (that's the bit behind the goal posts) must be between 22 metres and 10 metres. Pitch sizes for younger age groups vary.

How High and Wide are the Goal Posts?

They are 5.6 metres apart and the crossbar (the bar that the ball must go over) is 3 metres high. The posts are usually 15 metres high.

Rugby Made Simple

How Long is a Match?

A maximum of two periods of 40 minutes with a half time break of 10 minutes. Injury time will be added at the end. Younger players will have shorter matches.

How Does a Game Begin?

The captains toss a coin. The winner either chooses an end or chooses to kick off. At the start and after half time the game begins with a drop kick by any player of the team awarded the kick-off. The ball must be kicked in the direction of the opponents' ten metre line.

What is a "Dead Ball"?

The ball is "dead" when it is out of play – either it's gone out of the playing area (over the touchline or over the dead-ball line behind the goal posts) or there has been a try or the referee blows his whistle for an infringement.

When is a Ball "In Touch"?

The ball is "in touch" when it goes over the touchline (that's the boundary line down the sides) either by being kicked, knocked or carried over.

Who are the Officials and What Do They Do?

There are three officials, the referee and two touch judges. The referee is the only judge of fact and law (something which excitable spectators and argumentative players find hard to accept). The touch judges carry a flag which they hold up to show where the ball went into touch. They also stand behind the goalposts to see if a goal has been scored. If it has, they will raise their flag.

What are "Sevens"?

It's a variation of rugby union with just seven players in each team. Generally a faster, more exciting game to watch but the matches are shorter. It originated in Melrose, Scotland and is usually played during the summer months. It's now a recognised Olympic sport and will make its debut in 2016.

Why is Rugby League different?

Good question but it's a long and complicated answer which is beyond the scope of this book. The main differences relate to tackling (in rugby league play is stopped when a player is tackled), types of permitted tackle and scoring.

Chapter Eleven
A Brief History of Rugby Union

Tradition holds that rugby was invented at Rugby School in the 1820s when a schoolboy called William Webb Ellis "with a fine disregard for the rules of football as played in his time, first took the ball in his arms and ran with it". In fact it is highly unlikely that there were any firm rules for football as it was the boys rather than their teachers who made the rules and they frequently changed with each new intake of boys. Rules changes, such as the legality of carrying or running with the ball, were often agreed shortly before the commencement of a game.

At the time William Webb Ellis picked up the ball different forms of football, (many of which were similar to rugby) were being played throughout the world. The survival and dominance of this particular version is attributable to three of the schoolboys who decided to codify and publish a set of rules in 1845. These constituted the first written rules for any form of "football". Thus the game of Rugby Union was born.

Until the late 1860s rugby was played with a leather ball with an inner-tube made of a pig's bladder. The shape of the bladder made the ball slightly oval but they were far more spherical in shape than they are today. With the introduction of rubber bladders there was a gradual flattening of the ball over the years as the emphasis of the game moved towards handling and away from kicking. In 1892 the RFU included compulsory dimensions for the ball for the first time.

The first international rugby match was played between Scotland and England at Raeburn Place, Edinburgh, the home ground of Edinburgh Academicals (which was the first rugby club to be formed in Scotland), on 27 March 1871. The match was narrowly won by Scotland. Prior to this date three Scotland/England fixtures had been played but they were not considered true internationals as the Scottish team included London players who claimed a Scottish connection.

By the end of the 19th century rugby union had spread far and wide principally within the British Empire but also beyond it. Australia, New Zealand and South Africa embraced the game with enthusiasm.

The Five Nations Championships began in 1910 with England, Scotland, Ireland, Wales and France playing each other in the same season. Italy joined the Five Nations in 2000 making an annual Six Nations Championship.

The most important club competition is the European Rugby Champions Cup tournament which began in 1995. Leading club teams in each of the six rugby nations (ie club teams from England, Scotland, France, Ireland, Wales and Italy) play each other annually.

The first Rugby World Cup was played in 1987 and continues to be played every four years between the top international teams. The winner is awarded the William Webb Ellis Cup. The first country to host the event was New Zealand. England will host the event in 2015 and Japan will host it in 2019. The tournament is run by the International Rugby Board, the sport's international governing body.